21st Century Skills Library

ROAD TO RECOVERY

AMERICAN ALLIGATOR

Susan H. Gray

Cherry Lake Publishing
Ann Arbor, Michigan

Published in the United States of America by Cherry Lake Publishing
Ann Arbor, MI
www.cherrylakepublishing.com

Content Adviser: Dr. Harold K. Voris, Curator and Head, Amphibians and Reptiles, Department of Zoology, The Field Museum, Chicago, Illinois

*Cherry Lake Publishing would like to acknowledge the work of
The Partnership for 21st Century Skills.
Please visit www.21stcenturyskills.org for more information.*

TABLE of CONTENTS

CHAPTER ONE

GETTING THE GIRL

Alligators blow bubbles under the water as part of their mating ritual.

A huge male alligator heads for the water. The weather is warming up,

and he's looking for a mate. He hauls his 900-pound (408-kilogram) body

into the swamp and bellows with all his might. Three females take notice, and one swims toward him. The male slowly lifts his head, tilts it back, then slams it down onto the water. The enormous splash sends water, frogs, and twigs flying everywhere.

To attract a mate, this alligator raises his neck out of the water.

21st Century Content

The river was so crowded with alligators that "it would have been easy to have walked across on their heads." So wrote the U.S. naturalist and explorer named William Bartram in the 1770s. Bartram was in Florida, studying the plants and animals of the St. Johns River. He could not believe how many different flowers, birds, and fish lived there. But he was especially impressed with the alligators. Only two counties on Earth have alligators: the United States and China. The Chinese alligator is also endangered.

Alligators are cold-blooded animals. This does not mean that their blood is cold. It means that their body temperature goes up and down with the outside temperature. What effect do you think the weather has on the alligator's behavior?

This is just what the female is looking for. She paddles up alongside the male and bumps him with her snout. He rubs his throat along her back. Then they take turns lowering their heads and blowing bubbles underwater. It's spring and time for courtship in the swamp.

Alligator courtship takes place in areas of open water.

CHAPTER TWO

AN ALLIGATOR'S LIFE

*Nostrils at the top of the head allow an alligator to breathe
while it is almost completely submerged in the water.*

Alligators have roamed swampy areas of North America for millions of

years. In fact, scientists believe they lived at the same time as the dinosaurs.

These animals are survivors.

Alligators prefer to live in still water.

Today, American alligators (scientific name *Alligator mississippiensis*) live in wet lowlands in the southeastern United States. They can be found in lakes, swamps, marshes, and slow-moving rivers. They do not live in the salty water of the ocean.

Alligators are the biggest reptiles in North America. Females can grow more than 9 feet (2.7 meters) long. Males can stretch out to more than 14 feet (4.3 m). The largest males weigh about 1,000 pounds (454 kg).

The bodies of males and females are black or greenish black and are covered in armor. Bony plates are embedded in the skin on the back. The belly is a lighter color and is covered with tough scales. The muscular tail is as long as the rest of the body. Four stocky legs splay out to the sides.

American alligators are built to be predators. With huge mouths and more than 70 teeth, they can easily kill and devour smaller animals. The eyes and nostrils are at the top of the head. This allows an alligator to breathe and keep a lookout while its body is hidden underwater. When a bird, fish, raccoon, or other animal wanders too close, the alligator snatches it with surprising speed. An alligator swallows small animals in

Alligators usually eat small animals, such as fish, snakes, and turtles.

one gulp. It holds larger animals between its jaws and thrashes about or

spins its body until the **prey** is torn into smaller pieces.

When they reach about 10 years of age, males begin to look for mates.

In the springtime, they bellow to attract females. They may also show off their throats and slam their heads down on the water. Once a pair comes together, they will nudge each other, bump snouts, and blow bubbles. These activities can go on for hours.

Before a female lays her eggs, she scouts out a nesting place. The best spots are those that rise up out of the water. Once she finds a good place, she uses her snout and legs to shove mud and dead plants into a heap. The heaps are huge—up to 10 feet (3 m) across.

The female then scoops out a bowl in the top of the heap. She lays between 20 and 50 eggs in the bowl. To keep the eggs warm and safe, she covers them with mud and plants from the mound. As the plants rot, they give off heat.

The warmth of the mound is very important to the developing alligators. If eggs stay at less than 85 degrees Fahrenheit (29 degrees Celsius), the hatchlings will be females. If eggs stay above 91°F (33°C), the young alligators will be males. Eggs that remain between these temperatures will produce a mix of males and females.

In late summer, about 65 days after she lays her eggs, the mother hears hoarse chirping sounds coming from the nest. These are the baby alligators about to hatch. She scrapes the mud and dead plants away just in time to see her babies cracking through their eggs.

Each baby is about as long as a marking pen. It is black, like its parents. It also has yellow stripes around its body. These stripes disappear over time.

As the babies hatch, the mother gathers up groups of them in her mouth. Then she carries them down to the water. There she opens her mouth and gently sways her head back and forth. This gets the little alligators to jump out and take their first swim.

It takes about six years for a young alligator to reach adulthood.

Young alligators stick close to their mothers for at least a year. Alligator mothers are very protective. They have to be. Raccoons, bobcats, snakes, and birds love to eat tender little alligators.

As the young ones grow, they begin to act more and more like adults. They learn to catch bugs, snails, frogs, and small fish. When they are larger, they start to dig trenches and to make "gator holes." To make a hole, an alligator swishes its snout and tail to scoop out a pit in the mud. The more it swishes, the deeper the pit becomes. When it rains, the pit fills with water. During dry periods, alligators survive by staying in their own pools.

Alligators are great survivors for many reasons. The babies have very watchful mothers. The young ones learn to be excellent predators. The older ones dig holes so they have their own water supplies. In

Unlike adults, young alligators have yellow stripes on their tales.

The alligator family includes the American alligator and the Chinese alligator. The Chinese alligator is only about half the size of its American cousin. Its nickname in Chinese is *Tu Long* or "muddy dragon."

the wild, alligators will often reach 50 years of age. In

captivity, they can live to be 80!

CHAPTER THREE

ALLIGATORS IN DANGER

American alligators have been on Earth for millions of years. They have developed all sorts of tricks to help them survive. Mothers fiercely protect their young, and no other animal dares to attack an adult. However, at one time, the creature almost became extinct. What happened?

Alligators have between 74 and 80 teeth. If they lose a tooth, a new one grows in its place.

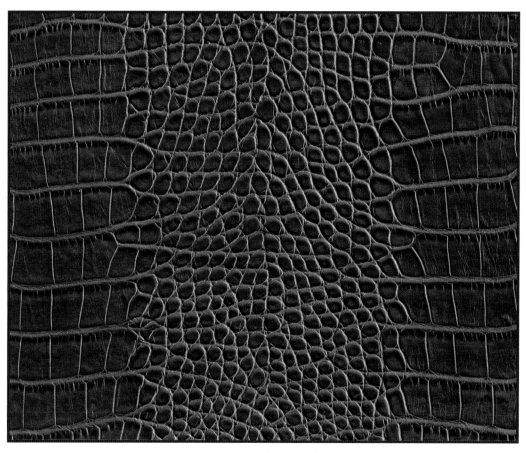

Many people prize alligator skins for their unique texture.

In the 1800s, many people began to notice what a valuable hide the

alligator had. The skin of its underside could be made into beautiful shoes,

purses, and belts. Alligator boots and wallets became very popular. People

The skin on an alligator's back is rough with bony plates that protect it.

across Europe and the United States wanted more and more of these items.

So hunters killed thousands of alligators for their skins.

In the meantime, others hunted the alligator for its meat. And still others killed the animal simply because they didn't want it around. During this same time, the population of the United States was growing. More and more people were moving into the alligators' territory. Homes and businesses were going up in areas that used to be swamplands. The alligators' habitat—its natural home—was disappearing. This went on for years. By 1960, the alligator population was dangerously low.

21st Century Content

The alligator got its name from early Spanish explorers in North America. They called it *el largato*, meaning "the lizard." Over time, the name changed to *allagarter*, then to *alligator*.

CHAPTER FOUR

THINGS GET BETTER

*Both federal and state governments set aside
land where alligators could live.*

State officials finally saw that they had to protect the alligators. In

Alabama, Florida, Louisiana, and Texas, it became illegal to hunt them.

In 1967, the U.S. government decided to help. The government named the American alligator an endangered species. This meant that it was in

danger of disappearing altogether.

Unfortunately, this didn't help much. In some states, hunting was

still legal. In others, hunters would sneak out at night to shoot the

animals. Also, there were no laws against buying and selling skins.

*American alligator numbers began to increase in
some areas after hunting was restricted.*

So the government got tougher. New laws made it illegal to hunt alligators anywhere, and it became a crime to buy or sell the hides.

Finally, things began to improve. In 1977, the government said the alligator was no longer endangered in parts of three states—Florida,

Alligators in backyards and on roads have become a more common sight as homes are built near alligator habitats.

Texas, and Louisiana. This is where most alligators lived. About 10 years later, the government said the alligator was no longer endangered in *any* state.

New problems have come up, however. Every year, there are more and more alligators. They are slowly spreading out into new areas. There are also more and more people living near the alligators' habitat. Today, people and alligators are more likely than ever before to see each other.

As a result, law enforcement officers get thousands of calls about alligators every year. People are reporting them in their driveways and backyards. Some call to say that an alligator attacked their pet

Sometimes it is important to think carefully about stories before believing them. For years, people have told stories about alligators living beneath New York City. They say that New Yorkers bought baby alligators during their vacations in Florida. When the babies grew too big, the owners flushed them down the toilet. The tiny reptiles grew up roaming through miles and miles of sewer pipes, feeding on rats. There's only one thing wrong with the story. It's not true. Alligators need warmth and decent water to live. No alligator could survive in a sewer.

or a family member. The number of reports goes up every year. The number of injuries from alligator attacks also goes up.

Unfortunately, some people like to feed the alligators. Others just like to see how near they can come to the reptiles without getting hurt. They ignore the fact that alligators are meat-eating animals.

When the reptiles have too much contact with people, they lose their fear of humans. They begin to approach people, expecting food. Of course, this ends in disaster. In some states, it is now illegal to feed the animals.

CHAPTER FIVE

SAFE FOR NOW

Today, American alligators are no longer endangered. In fact, there are more than 3 million alligators in the southeastern United States. They live in wet, marshy areas from North Carolina to Texas, including states such as Arkansas and Oklahoma.

People who live near alligator habitats have to be careful around the animals.

Hunting is now legal in some states. Hunting helps to keep the alligator numbers under control. However, the laws are very strict. The hunting season might be only a few days long. Hunters may take only a certain number of alligators each season. Plus, they must report every alligator they take.

Some people prefer other ways of getting alligators. To obtain meat and

Alligator farms have helped cut down on illegal hunting.

hides, they have started alligator farms. They raise

thousands of alligators and return some of them to

the wild.

People who find alligator eggs on their land

can sell them to these farmers. This is good for

the alligators.

In 2005, landowners sold more than half a

million eggs. Then two big hurricanes hit, destroying

many alligators' homes and nests. Fortunately, the

eggs that had already been collected were saved from

the storms.

This legal harvesting of alligator eggs also

provides a good reason for landowners to maintain

Everglades National Park covers a large part of southern Florida. The park is protected and maintained by the National Park Service. It has marshes, islands, grassy plains, and forests. More than 300 different kinds of birds and more than 50 different kinds of reptiles live there. American alligators thrive in the Everglades. Crocodiles and caimans live there as well.

Life & Career Skills

In Florida, many professors and students study alligators. They are working together to learn more about alligator behavior and the best ways to protect the habitat. When these researchers learn something new, they share it with the government. This flow of information helps keep strong laws in place to protect the American alligator.

Collecting eggs has been one strategy for helping alligator populations recover.

wetlands. The disappearance of their marshy habitat is still a threat to the alligators.

Although their numbers have bounced back, alligators are still protected. Thanks to many people, the American alligator will be with us for years to come.

This map shows where the American alligator lives in the United States.

GLOSSARY

caimans (KAY-muhnz) members of the alligator family that live in Central and South America

captivity (kap-TIH-vih-tee) the condition of not being able to roam freely

cold-blooded (KOHLD BLUHD-id) having a body temperature that goes up and down with the outside temperature

courtship (KORT-ship) behavior or activities that lead to mating

extinct (ek-STINGT) no longer living

gharials (GARE-ee-uhlz) alligator-like animals that live in India

hatchlings (HATCH-leengz) animals that have recently hatched from eggs

predators (PREH-duh-terz) animals that hunt and eat other animals

prey (PRAY) an animal that is eaten by another animal

reptiles (REP-tylz) cold-blooded animals that are covered with plates or scales

species (SPEE-sheez) a group of similar animals or plants

FOR MORE INFORMATION

Books

Rockwell, Anne. *Who Lives in an Alligator Hole?* New York: Collins, 2006.

Snyder, Trish. *Alligator and Crocodile Rescue: Changing the Future for Endangered Wildlife.* Richmond Hill, ON: Firefly Books, 2006.

Staub, Frank J. *Alligators.* Minneapolis: Lerner Publications, 1995.

Web Sites

Everglades National Park: Alligators
www.nps.gov/archive/ever/eco/gator.htm
For more information about the average size, age,
weight, and speed of the American alligator

Florida Fish and Wildlife Conservation Commission: My FWC.com
www.floridaconservation.org/gators/kids.htm
To send a question to an alligator expert

The World Almanac for Kids: Alligator
www.worldalmanacforkids.com/EXPLORE/animals/alligator.html
To find an animals directory and information about American alligators

INDEX

ABOUT THE AUTHOR

Susan H. Gray has a master's degree in zoology. She has written more than 70 science and reference books for children and especially loves writing about animals. Gray also likes to garden and play the piano. She lives in Cabot, Arkansas, with her husband, Michael, and many pets.